More power to you

GUIDES TO GROWTH

More power to you

LEE HASTINGS BRISTOL, JR.

Word Books, Publisher

Waco, Texas

More Power to You

Other Books by Lee H. Bristol, Jr.

Hymns for Children & Grownups
    (with Harold Friedell)
    Farrar, Straus & Young, 1952
Feast of the Star
    A Pageant for Epiphany
    (with Harold Friedell)
    H. W. Gray Division, Belwin Mills Co., 1956
Seed for a Song
    the biography of Bishop Robert Nelson Spencer
    Little, Brown & Company, 1958
Developing the Corporate Image
    Charles Scribner's Sons, 1960
    (Japanese edition)
    Yomiur RV Hose, Ltd., Japan, 1971
Songs from Luke (Junior Choir)
    E. C. Kerby, Ltd., Toronto
Songs from Matthew (Junior Choir)
    E. C. Kerby, Ltd., Toronto
Thirty-Five Sacred Rounds & Canons
    from Four Centuries
    E. C. Kerby, Ltd., Toronto
New Songs for the Junior Choir
    (with Harold Friedell)
    Concordia Publishing House, 1961
Let the Children Sing (Junior Choir)
    Abingdon Press

The Bristol Collection
    Contemporary Hymn Tune Preludes for Organ
    Volumes I, II, and III
    Harold Flammer Division, Shawnee Press
More Hymns & Spiritual Songs
    Authorized Supplement to the Episcopal
    Hymnal
    (General Editor)
    Walton Music Corporation, 1972
The Big Picnic and other New Testament Meals
    John Knox Press, 1975

Contents

Foreword

Lee H. Bristol, Jr., is a layman who practices what he preaches. A talented musician and hymnologist, a business executive and an academic administrator, he is first of all a Christian of deep conviction and enormous gifts and dedication. He is in demand at home and in England as a speaker and preacher because of the fresh insights he has into the resources of the faith for daily living and his unique ability to communicate with his contemporaries.

More Power to You is a handbook for Christian living. It is inspired by the conviction that the Christian faith makes a difference in the quality of the life one lives and the work he accomplishes. The chapters deal with the worth of the human person, caring and responding, how one relates to God and his fellows, and how one fulfills his vocation. There is not a trite word or thought in the book. The author chooses the right illustration, usually taken from daily life, to illuminate the deepest spiritual truth.

There is a continuing need for the theologian who clarifies the meaning of the gospel and its relevance for the problems of today. There is a continuing need for the clergyman who proclaims this gospel for us men and our salvation. But seldom has there been a greater need than now for the layman who lives out his faith in daily commerce and is willing to share it with others who are seeking depth and meaning in their lives. Dr. Bristol is such a layman, and *More Power to You* is such a book.

JAMES I. McCORD
President
Princeton Theological Seminary

Acknowledgments

The frontispiece is a reproduction of "The Return of the Prodigal Son," an etching by Jean-Louis Forain (1852-1931). Reprint by permission of the Cincinnati Art Museum, Eden Park, Cincinnati, Ohio 45202. Mr. and Mrs. Ross W. Sloniker Collection of Twentieth Century Biblical and Religious Prints.

Chapters One and Two include material by the author which appeared in *Forward Day by Day* (Forward Movement Publications) and *The Episcopalian* magazine. Used by permission.

Chapter Five includes one stanza from "Dear Lord and Father of Mankind." Used by permission of Houghton Mifflin Company.

Chapter Eight: quotation from *A Life to Live, A Way to Pray* by John B. Coburn (Seabury Press, 1973). Used by permission.

Chapter Nine: quotation from *The Story of Jesus* by Theodore Parker Ferris (Oxford University Press, 1953). Used by permission.

Chapter Ten: quotation from *A Life to Live, A Way to Pray* by John B. Coburn (Seabury Press, 1973). Used by permission. Quotation from *Mark-*

Introduction

This is a book by a layman, a theological amateur, written for other lay men and women seeking a firmer grasp on matters of faith and a deepening of their spiritual lives. It is the work of a churchman who has had experience working with other lay persons in the secular worlds of business, education, and the arts.

If, in outlining steps I have found helpful in my own life, I seem to imply that it is we alone who do the trick by pulling ourselves up by our own bootstraps, don't you believe it! Nothing is further from the truth. It is only the Holy Spirit working within us who can bring us ever closer to God's highest expectation for our lives.

This book is not intended to provide the final answer or a last word. I hope it will prove to be a springboard from which you can develop further a still better spiritual program of your own.

Since this book is a labor of love on the part of the author, I have asked that any royalties be assigned to the Trinity Counseling Service of Princeton, New

Jersey, an interdenominational agency devoted to many of the objectives which prompted this book.

In World War II, our post chaplain, Colonel John Williamson, used to close services with a prayer I feel appropriate for the beginning of this book:

Thanks and praise be unto thee, Almighty God. Keep us, thy servants, O Heavenly Father, in all our ways, and may we so live that men may take knowledge of us, that we have been with Jesus. Amen.

LEE H. BRISTOL, JR.
Princeton, New Jersey

A Prayer for Grace

O God, whose blessed Son asked "What do ye more than others?", grant us grace so to follow him in love and service at home, at work, and out in the community that we radiate the kind of difference which may draw others to him; through Jesus Christ our Lord. Amen.

1

What Difference
Does It Make?

CARL JUNG, the Swiss psychiatrist, tells of a woman
who came to see him and poured out her problems,
real and imaginary, at great length. Finally, she
looked up and said, "You know, doctor, if I could
just feel my life counted for something in terms of
the lives of others, you and I wouldn't have to sit
around and have all this silly talk about my nerves!"

I suspect all of us are like that woman at times.
We would like to feel our lives really counted for
something. Dostoevsky once said that all one had to
do to kill a person's spirit was to give his or her
work the character of meaninglessness.

As Christians we have certain spiritual resources
to combat this feeling of meaninglessness. We are
bound to have our ups and downs, but we do not

have to do it alone. Jesus did not leave us with a book and a list of principles to follow; he left himself —his Spirit—to help us.

Spiritual growth is not easy; we laymen find it frustrating at times. But our faith should make a difference.

When an American bishop went to Russia several years ago, he attended a number of church services. After one of these, a young girl came up to him and asked all about the church in America. The bishop gave her as complete a picture as he could. Then the girl, with sincerity and no trace of sarcasm, asked, "But what difference does it make? What difference does it make in the people?"

Quite a question, isn't it? Disarming and strangely reminiscent of one Jesus raised in the Sermon on the Mount: "What do ye more than others?" (Matt. 5:47). I don't think Jesus was interested in the number of things a person did but rather in the quality of spirit a person brought to what he did. We know, for example, that he could get very angry with the Pharisees who indulged in any number of religious practices, and yet he could be compassionate with a prostitute who had a change of heart and wanted to start a new kind of life. Not quantity but quality concerns our Lord; not what we claim our faith to be but how much that faith has changed us.

20

Isn't the acid test of a faith, after all, how much it changes us? Do we radiate a difference where we live and move and have our being? If we are not different husbands and wives and parents, if we are not different business and professional people, if we don't meet awkward situations differently because of what we believe, does our faith really mean very much?

You and I profess and call ourselves Christians. We attend services and take part in church activities. We see that our children are baptized and that they go to church school on Sundays. But, as the Russian girl put it, what difference does it make?

Take the home, for example. Why is it that there seems to be little or no difference between the Christian home and any other? I am not just speaking here of the way many so-called Christian homes may be without family prayer, regular Bible reading, or grace at meals. I am speaking about how members of a Christian family treat one another—husband, wife, parents, and children.

Haven't you known married couples who seemed to lead two separate lives with no attempt to share each other's concerns? Haven't you watched families eating at a restaurant and noticed how often children seem to have trouble getting their parents —especially their fathers—to listen to them?

It is easy to let outside interests or being overtired cause us to be inconsistent or unfair with our children. It is easy to make demands on our families which were never made on us. It is easy to forget even just to listen to one another! The Christian answer lies not necessarily in giving up more time to our children or wife or husband; it seems to me, much of the answer lies in what we do with the time we give.

Shortly before the famous lawyer Joseph Welch died, his son told him, "Dad, when we were growing up, your most influential moments were your most inadvertent ones. We were apt to imitate what you really were, not what you said you were, or even what you may have believed you were."

How can one be the perfect parent or husband or wife? We Christians don't know all the answers, but I like to think our faith gives us a keener sense of unquestioning responsibility to our families, to those at home who often look at us as if to ask, "What do ye more than others?"

Or take the world of our daily work. We know our faith has much to do with our jobs. The Bible mentions work about a thousand times. The Scriptures teach us that our Lord called all of us, laymen and clergy alike, to be his ambassadors to the world. And, quite frankly, just what do most of us do about it on the job? All work can be sacred, not just what we do in church on Sundays. What we do on the job becomes sacred or secular in terms of the spirit we bring to it.

The other day, a woman I know telephoned Grand Central Station for information and was surprised at the courtesy and helpfulness of the man on the other end of the line. "My, but you're helpful!" she said.

"I try to be," said the man, with conviction.

My friend was intrigued. "What is your position?" she asked.

"Oh, I'm just a dispatcher. You might say my job is giving out information, but I like to think it's more than that. I like to think my job is trying to make travel easier and pleasanter for people. Guess it's all in the way you look at it."

I think he's right. It *is* all in the way you look at it. "For some clergy, work is a chore; for some cab drivers, work is a ministry."

Living our faith on the job may not mean instituting hymn-sings at the coffee break—chances are we might meet with a little sales resistance! But it may very well mean seeing the sacred side of situations which others overlook—like how human beings may be affected by that proposed layoff or whether your company's services are everything that your ads claim them to be.

What matters is not how many committees a Christian is on but what he brings to the committee he *is* on. Someone once wrote in the *Harvard Business Review* that our Lord is not so much concerned with whether you're the board chairman or the night watchman as he is concerned with what kind of person just happens to be chairman or night watchman.

I do not mean, of course, to suggest that it is always easy to see the sacred side of work. Often our work will seem dreary, mechanical, meaningless. At such times we must remind ourselves that no matter how routine or boring a job may seem, it still gives us the opportunity to serve God—if not in the work itself, at least in the way it offers us a chance to touch the lives of those working to our right and to our left.

I do not think we hope for the kind of man I know who owns a small business and literally compels his employees to attend a prayer meeting first thing each morning. I like to think we are more interested in someone like a sales manager I once knew. He had to fly out to the Coast to reprimand severely one of his salesmen. After he had done so, he remained in the man's territory for three weeks to see how the man survived. Would he fold, or would he pick himself up and start over, a better person? The story in this case had a happy ending, but its significance to me lay in the fact that here was a man who saw the job of sales manager as the kind of ministry it certainly can be. He cared about the people who worked for him.

Living one's faith on the job is not easy. Many of the decisions a Christian faces in his work are not black or white or clear-cut. It is difficult and confusing to face decisions in the gray areas. Is it worth the risk to disagree with the boss? Wouldn't it be easier just this once to go along? The Christian's faith will give him a sense of responsibility to those related to him, a sense of responsibility that helps him face up squarely to such questions.

Day in and day out, consciously or unconsciously, there are those where we work who look at us in situations on the job as if to ask, "What do ye more than others?"

But it is not enough that a Christian tries to be a good husband or wife or parent, important as this may be. It is not enough that he tries to live his faith on the job. Above and beyond what he does at home and at work, the Christian should recognize his unending responsibility to serve his community.

He views his community differently. He doesn't say, "I pay taxes. I give to the hospital and the United Fund. Let me alone!" He is deeply conscious of his responsibility to the others who make up his community. He knows the wisdom of the old Toc H motto, "Service is the rent we pay for our place on earth," and he knows too that community problems can be so complex these days that they call for joint effort. He may well have seen for himself how the same number of concerned citizens working in proper collaboration can often achieve far greater results than the same number of citizens working independently. Scientists call this potentiation; you and I might call it a kind of two plus two equals five proposition. As the late William Temple once said, "Nine-tenths of the work of the church in the world is done by Christians fulfilling responsibilities and performing tasks which in themselves are not part of the official system of the church at all."

"Seek ye first the kingdom of God and his righteousness" was not a call for us to go out of this world. It was a call to stay in this world but to see it differently, sensitized to needs which others overlook, putting first things first. This may mean working for just laws, helping the poor, or simply bringing people together. The opportunities are limitless. The service a Christian performs in his community may be the same as that of an agnostic "do-gooder." The difference lies in the Christian's motive—a grateful sense of concern, mutual responsibility, love, knowing that our Lord is counting on us and not having the heart to let him down. We profess and call ourselves Christians. What difference does it make? What do *we* more than others?

A young mother I know had to grow spiritually when illness hit her suddenly. She prayed for strength, and that prayer was answered, not only with strength for herself but a kind of strength she was able to pass along to others. Even her little boy noticed the change. "I don't know what's happened to you, Mommy," he said, "but you're different. You're different, and I think it's wonderful!"

With God's help we can manage to move off dead center and radiate a difference.

A Prayer for Trustfulness

O most loving Father, who willest us to give thanks for all things, to dread nothing but the loss of thee, and to cast all our care on thee, who carest for us; Preserve us from faithless fears and worldly anxieties, and grant that no clouds of this mortal life may hide from us the light of that love which is immortal, and which thou hast manifested unto us in thy Son, Jesus Christ our Lord. Amen.

—William Bright
(1824-1901)

2

Does Anyone Care
about You?

WALLACE SPEERS, a businessman, was standing in
New York's Penn Station one Friday afternoon when
an unshaven ex-convict walked up to him and said,
"You look friendly," and proceeded to tell him the
sad story of his life.

When he finished, he looked at Mr. Speers for a
moment. "Will you do something for me?" he asked.
"You know, there's not a soul in the world who cares
if I live or die. Would you mind thinking about me
for a couple of weeks? If I could know there was
someone somewhere thinking about me as a human
being, why—it would be worth a million dollars to
me."

With that, the man slipped into the crowd. Mr.

Speers started after him, but the man had disappeared.

"I've been haunted by that man's loneliness ever since," Mr. Speers later told a friend. "How many others there must be like him, lonely and unloved, in the crowds we see every day!"

The desire to feel someone cares about you is not peculiar to a lonely man in a railroad station. It haunts all of us—from the little boy watching his classmates choose up sides for a game in the school-yard to the old man in the sanitarium who rolls his wheelchair over to the window during visiting hours to see if that hoped-for car will turn in the drive-way. Deep within each of us is the continuing hope that someone somewhere really cares.

But isn't it true that caring is a two-way street? Those who care most for us are often those we first cared for ourselves. They are the ones to whom you gave something of yourself—the teen-agers you spent time with when nobody else did, the widow you made sure you included in neighborhood get-togethers, your son when you gave him the car keys and the chance to learn for himself the lessons of such freedom.

Caring expresses itself in many forms. When the occasion demands it, it may mean being severe with someone you wish to help. It may mean listening patiently to long complaints from a sickbed. It may mean deliberately letting a child learn the hard lesson of taking a beating from a schoolmate when you want to rush out and yell stop. It may mean just a wink to a loved one across a crowded room.

Check yourself on how much you care about others by answering these questions: When I pass a friend on the street, do I wait to be spoken to or am I first to speak? How do I look upon those I meet casually—newsboys, taxi drivers, store clerks? Do I see them merely as functionaries or as human beings who just happen to be newsboys, taxi drivers, or store clerks? One Rhode Island housewife says she regularly asks herself, "Is the delivery boy glad to leave packages at my door?"

It is not difficult to care about someone close to you, but what about people who wouldn't normally interest you, people to whom you are not naturally drawn? Is it possible to care for them?

At this point the spiritual person stands out from the crowd. His faith is a dynamic for caring; it sensitizes him to the needs and concerns of others. Faith helps him to love the unlovable. The more people he treats with kindness, the more people he seems to find himself liking in all walks of life. God's spirit working in such a man enables him to see in others something of what God sees in them.

"We love, because he first loved us," says the First Epistle of John. The heart of the Christian gospel is that God cares for us even when we forget him. In our need he continues to care for us in much the same way that a human parent loves his son as much when he flunks an exam as when he passes it with flying colors.

Lucy Caldwell, our neighbor, is the widow of Charlie Caldwell, the late football coach of Princeton University. After the death of her husband, Lucy was determined not to sit around and feel sorry for herself. So she went overseas to Vietnam to do volunteer work among the Marines who were fighting there.

One day at the Marine hospital, a medical officer asked Lucy to see if she could cheer up a young Marine who had been blinded by shrapnel. Nobody could get him to speak.

Lucy talked to the blinded Marine for some time before he finally opened up and told her, "I have a wife and little boy back in Ohio. I guess now that I am sightless, they'll be shipping me home to them soon . . ."

They talked at length and Lucy returned to visit him several times. Not long afterward, the Marine was sent home. It was not until about eighteen months later that Lucy heard from him again, this time through a letter dictated to his wife.

"Lucy," he wrote, "I thought you might like to know we now have a little girl. She's named Lucy after someone neither of us has ever seen."

Jesus makes it clear that when a man comes to judgment, he will not be asked what committees he was on or what kind of write-up he boasted in *Who's Who* or what title was painted on his office door. He will be asked, instead, what he did about the hungry, the thirsty, the homeless, prisoners perhaps, the physically handicapped. He will be asked what he did with the other chair in the living room or that extra place at the table or those leftovers in the kitchen or clothes that hung unused on hangers in the closet.

Bishop Frederick Warnecke tells the story of a lonely man who felt so rejected by the cold city in which he lived that he decided to kill himself by throwing himself in the river. As he left his room, he told himself, "If I meet someone on the street whose eyes catch mine, who somehow takes notice of me as a human being, I'll turn back. Only then." So he began his long walk across town to the river.

Here the story ends. But it poses the question, Had he met *you* on the street, would he have turned back?

Sir Wilfred Grenfell, the great medical missionary, used to tell this true story about a man who cared.

It was a cold night up at the front line trenches in the First World War. A guard officer was touring the various sentry posts when he came upon one guard asleep at his post. Of course, this is a terribly serious offense, especially in wartime. The guard was liable for general court martial.

The officer noticed that the poor sentry could hardly answer him, his teeth were chattering so. Then he noticed the boy didn't have an overcoat; so he took off his own coat and wrapped it around him and proceeded on his tour of the other sentries. It was a bitter cold night, and when the officer finally reached the guardhouse, he had caught a severe chill, a chill that later developed into pneumonia and from which he ultimately died.

The day the officer died, he was in a delirium. A friend was at his side and heard him say, "I see a man walking toward me. He looks familiar. He looks like Jesus Christ. He *is* Jesus, and I see he is wearing my overcoat."

Does anybody care about you or me? The Christian answer is a resounding yes, but the more relevant question is, Do we who profess and call ourselves Christians care enough *not* to let him down?

A Prayer for True Religion

Lord of all power and might, who art the author and giver of all good things; graft in our hearts the love of thy Name, increase in us true religion, and nourish us with all goodness, and of thy great mercy keep us in the same; through Jesus Christ our Lord. Amen.

—Gelasian Sacramentary

3

More Power to You

ALL OF US occasionally confront problems that seem
to force us to redirect our lives. It may be illness,
financial reverses, or the betrayal of friends.

The boss calls you in and tells you, "You're
through."

The police call to say, "Your son's in real trouble.
We need you down at headquarters at once."

Or the physician calls you in to tell you, "The
report is not good."

The message of the Christian gospel is not that
God will spare us such problems but rather that he
can give us the power to meet them head-on. Look
at Paul—stoned, beaten, shipwrecked three times,
spending a day and a night in the water, imprisoned
a number of times. Yet he was the first to admit God

did not ask him to endure more than God gave Paul the power to take.

A few years ago I saw evidence of this same power to "take it" in a Canadian prison. I met a remarkably cheerful prisoner, an inmate with great spiritual resources despite the depressing cell to which he was confined much of the time.

"How do you keep so cheerful cooped up, hour after hour, in this windowless cell?" I asked. "I'd get cabin fever if I had to stay here. I'll bet I'd flip!"

"Oh, it isn't easy," he admitted. "It's rough, but I make it a rule to remind myself of six or seven things each morning when I wake up: Everything could be worse. I still have my health. I still have friends who believe in me and care. My life is not over. I still have a chance to make something of myself. Feeling sorry for myself will get me nowhere. Being cheerful may help. So—I'll be cheerful, even when it hurts!" Over his bunk he had written words attributed to Sir Winston Churchill that said: "In this place there is no such thing as discouragement. Here it simply does not exist."

I doubt that God intends us to surrender ourselves, as some glib magazine writers suggest, in a sort of pass-the-buck-to-God way. I rather think God hopes we will seek his help in transforming the self he gave us in the first place, making us, as Paul puts it, "new creatures."

Some people seem able not only to face their problems but to go a step beyond. Some people seem to be able to take their problems, turn them around, and put them to work redemptively in the lives of others. I know some parents who lost a son in Vietnam. Later they were able to comfort neighbors who lost their son, and my friends somehow are strengthened themselves in the process of consoling others. An advertising executive was pinned under a burning car for hours and later rescued. The man underwent considerable plastic surgery. Later, he made countless trips to plastic surgery wards in city and military hospitals showing before-and-after pictures of what plastic surgery had done for him. His visits did much to give patients hope.

Such people have convinced me it is possible for the Christian, not only to find God's help in meeting problems head-on, but to learn to turn such problems around and use them to help others. After all, didn't Christ do this with his supreme suffering on the cross?

When we refer to the recorded miracles of Christ, most of us tend to think of his changing water into wine at Cana, feeding a hungry crowd on a hillside, giving sight to the blind, curing the sick. But the greatest miracle of all was the transformation of lives—Mary Magdalene, Andrew, Simon Peter, Saul of Tarsus. Through Jesus, ordinary people became extraordinary people.

This miracle still occurs today. I think, for example, of a ruthless business executive I met twenty years ago, interested only in making a fast buck. Today he is completely changed, self-giving to a fault, an executive interested in the growth of his associates by day, an after-hours volunteer in New York's Harlem area by night.

The story is told of a seemingly hopeless Yorkshire alcoholic, a miner who beat his wife and children and sold the furniture from his own house to buy more liquor. Finally, he left his family, lost his job, and appeared to be done for. A kindly vicar and two laymen took an interest in the man, attracted him to their local church. After many months, the man was converted and became a commited Christian. His friends helped him get his old job back at the mine, and the man began to use his pay check not only to support his family again but to replace the furniture he had sold to buy liquor.

One day, during a lunch-hour break at the mine, one of his fellow workers caught the man reading a pocket Testament. "You've got religion now," he said. "You're always reading the Bible. Tell me. You don't believe all that stuff about the miracles, do you? You know, turning water into wine at a wedding and feeding thousands from a few baskets of scraps?"

The man looked up from his reading. "I don't know about those," he said, "but I've seen Christ in my own life turn liquor into furniture, and that's miracle enough for me."

In effect God seems to say to us at times, "Unclench your fists. Turn palms upward, and let me take from you those elements that are holding you back and keeping you under the tyranny of self. Give me your strengths and weaknesses, your triumphs and failures, what you're proud of and what you're ashamed of about yourself. Let me give you a new self and enable you to become what all along I hoped you might be."

A Prayer for an Unconquered Heart

Give me, O Lord, a steadfast heart, which no unworthy affection may drag downwards; give me an unconquered heart, which no tribulation can wear out; give me an upright heart, which no unworthy purpose may tempt aside; through Jesus Christ our Lord. Amen.

—St. Thomas Aquinas
(ca. 1225-1274)

4

Really Beginning to Live

ALL OF US like to get information in a nutshell, in capsule form. We go in for instant-this and instant-that. I guess we are a lot like the lawyer who went up to Jesus and asked, "What do I have to do to know the abundant life you're talking about? What must I do to inherit eternal life?"

Jesus did not give him a direct answer. He did what lawyers often do to one another. He asked another question: "What does it say in the law, and how would you interpret it?"

The lawyer was probably taken aback, but he recited what he knew: "You shall love the Lord your God with all your heart, soul, and mind and your neighbor as yourself."

"Quite right," said Jesus. "Do this, and you will live."

The lawyer's answer was shorter than a standard night-letter telegram, less than two dozen words in fact, but, as Jesus put it, "On these two commandments hang all the others." *Do this, and you will live.*

The other day, two friends of mine got to discussing those commandments during their morning coffee break. Was man's chief and highest end to praise God or was it to improve the lot of his fellow-man?

"Bob," said one, "the two just cannot be separated."

"Precisely," said the other. One might say that the two commandments are like the two halves of a round-trip ticket: not good if detached. And the word *love* is the common denominator.

St. Augustine said of that first commandment—to love God with heart, soul, and mind—that if you really fulfill the first commandment the second will take care of itself, it will naturally flow from the first. "Love God, and do as you please."

It is easy to neglect prayer. In our jet-paced world we are tempted to minimize the importance of prayer and worship in our eagerness forever to be "doing things" or perhaps rushing off ill-prepared to try to improve the lot of our fellow-man.

Donald Coggan, the present archbishop of Canterbury, says, "When you try to get to know God and fulfill that first commandment, you may find him a far cry from the kind of God you used to cringe before when you thought your jet plane or the stock market might go down."

I heard Dr. Coggan remind a meeting of clergy in Virginia, "Chances are you will find God is a far cry from being a benign, easygoing grandfather who winks at whatever you do as if to suggest, 'A good time was had by all!'"

The world will constantly exert pressures to pull us away from God, to pull us downstream by flattery or by the "but everybody's doing it" syndrome. It will not be easy to head upstream, the other way, against the tide toward God, but he offers us a towline to grab hold of, a line that can help us turn around and lead redirected lives.

The Greek word for that turning around is *metanoia,* and it appears over and over again in the New Testament to describe turning away from a way of life that is negative, harmful, regimented, to a way of life that offers fulfillment, meaning, inner peace.

I read somewhere of Christ being compared to "the strong swimmer who carries the rope ashore and so not only secures his own position but makes possible rescue for all who follow." Paul had a lot to say about such a turning around in his own life, how he felt Christ completely took hold of his life, turned him around, and sent him off in a new direction.

When you and I grab hold of that towline, we may be surprised to find even our vocabulary changed from a non-Christian emphasis on the verb *to have* or the very American *to do* to the great Christian verb *to be*. The late Archbishop of Canterbury William Temple used to say, *"To be* is infinitely greater than *to do";* to be in Christ yourself is even greater than to preach the gospel.

The other day, I stopped for a traffic light opposite a neighborhood settlement house. While I was standing there, waiting for the light to change, I noticed the words of the second commandment carved in large letters all across the front of the building: Love your neighbor as yourself.

"Just who is my neighbor?" the lawyer asked.

Jesus' reply was, of course, the Parable of the Good Samaritan and what happened to a solitary traveler on the dangerous road from Jerusalem to Jericho which his hearers knew all too well. (One can imagine them saying to one another, "Anyone traveling alone on an unsafe road like that ought to have his head examined!")

Jesus told how the man was mugged and left

half-dead by the side of the road. Along came the priest, who passed by on the other side. (Archbishop Fulton Sheen told our vicar, "I'll bet that priest was on his way to a liturgical conference!") Next came the Levite. He, too, passed by on the other side— maybe a little like you and me at times when we skid out from under opportunities, saying, "Not just now," or "Let George do it," or "That sort of thing just isn't my bag."

Then along came a total stranger, the Samaritan, who poured wine and oil on the wounds of the injured man, bandaged them, carried the man on his own animal to an inn where he would be cared for. The Samaritan gave money to the innkeeper. "If this isn't enough," he said, "I'll give you the rest the next time I go this way."

We all know Good Samaritans today: the woman who does not just lend her name to a charity letterhead but actually involves herself in the work of that charity . . . the man who does not just write a sympathy letter to a friend who lost his wife but later, long after others seem to have forgotten, stops by to ask, "How are you getting along? Is there anything I can do to help?" I know of a man who learned that a poor neighbor was in danger of losing his eyesight. My friend went to New York, determined to persuade the finest eye surgeon to take the case. The neighbor's eyesight *was* saved, but, mysteriously, when the patient went to pay his bill, he found it had already been paid—anonymously.

But to love your neighbor means far more than just being kind to someone when he is in trouble. The late Theodore Ferris used to say, "It may mean standing up *for* him when he is misunderstood; it may mean standing up *to* him, being candidly frank, when he is mistaken."

The Quakers have a saying that is wonderfully appropriate for many of us who tend to spread ourselves too thin: "You cannot be crucified on every cross." When we remember the way Christ concentrated his attention on a few key persons, persons he felt would carry the word to others, we come to appreciate the wisdom of the Quaker words about "centering down" or focusing our attention in close-ups. Maybe a good morning prayer for all of us would be: "Lord, on whom and on what would you have me focus my attention today?"

The summary of the law is not a list of negatives or don'ts; it is a list of do's. As we capture a sense of wonder—about the tree outside the window we used to look at but now seldom see or stars in the sky overhead when we step out for a breath of air or the love you share with that dear person across the dinner table or the joy of just being alive, as we begin to see the world about us not with our own eyes but with those of Christ, we begin to understand why *love God* is the "first and great commandment."

Similarly, as we lose ourselves in others, not because we feel we *ought* to do so but rather because we really *want* to because we see in others something of what Christ sees in them, we will begin to recognize our Lord himself in those we befriend.

"Inasmuch as you did what you did to one of the least," said Jesus, "you did it to me." Love God with heart, soul, and mind—and your neighbor as yourself. "Do this," said Jesus, "and you will live." Down through the ages, the joyous saints say, "You'd better believe it, because it's true!"

A Prayer for Quiet Confidence

*O God of peace, who hast taught us that in return-
ing and rest we shall be saved, in quietness and
confidence shall be our strength; By the might of thy
Spirit left us, we pray thee to thy presence, where
we may be still and know that thou art God;
through Jesus Christ our Lord. Amen.*

—John W. Suter, Jr.

5

The Constructive Use
of Silence

"You've got to be kidding!" my children shouted
when I told them the title of this chapter. "You of
all people writing about silence!" I was not kidding.
Garrulous as I am, I am beginning to learn something of the virtues of silence.

The constructive use of silence, however, involves
more than the virtues of keeping one's mouth shut
—wise as that may be at times! My growing conviction is that no one can hope to progress very far
in terms of personal spiritual growth who does not
make some constructive use of silence. As a matter
of fact, no one who makes a practice of using silence constructively can fail, it seems to me, to find
himself or herself somewhat changed in the process.

Have you ever noticed how beautiful a word like

hush can be? Just saying the word *hush* helps one sense quiet, calm, peace. One of the most beloved prayers in the English language is one attributed to Cardinal Newman, "O Lord, support us all the day long in this troublous life, until the shadows lengthen and the evening comes and the busy world is hushed . . ."

Well, our busy world is not hushed very much of the time, is it? We hear the roar of jet planes overhead, pneumatic drills pounding incessantly at city pavements. We see nonchalant pedestrians walking along the streets with blaring radios slung over their shoulders. Or, back home, our children tell us, "I can't do my homework without it"—without the radio or TV or stereo blaring in the background.

I believe it was George Eliot who once wrote, "If we could hear the grass grow or the squirrel's heartbeat, we should die of the roar that lies on the other side of silence."

Some people who believe in the importance of silence have been an inspiration to me. One is the prominent organist of St. Alban's Abbey in England. When he was first sent a form to fill out for listing his name in the British *Who's Who*, he was asked his favorite recreation. He replied, "Finding a little silence." The editors thought he had made a mistake but soon discovered he meant what he said.

A New York magazine editor is such a believer in the constructive use of silence that he has founded what he calls the Unorganized League of Silence. There are no membership dues, no officers, no meetings to attend. You are automatically a member if you will agree to pause for three minutes at noon, shut out the distractions of the world around you, and try to listen to what God may have to say to you.

Did you know it is against the law to play transistor radios in most British parks? Up in Scotland at the Edinburgh Zoo, I actually saw a sign which said, "Thoughtful persons do not play transistor radios in public places. Others must not." Here in the United States I have seen juke boxes where you can actually buy silence. If you do not wish to hear a record, you can put in a dime to purchase five minutes of silence.

There are indeed people who value silence, and we can learn from them. Yet silence for its own sake is not necessarily a virtue. As a matter of fact, one might say some silences are bad. Take the case of a difficult marriage. Sometimes hurt feelings can come, not just from what is said, but from what is not said. Silence can be unkind. But I am concerned with the constructive use of silence—shutting out the sounds and distractions around us, if only for a few minutes, to listen for God and to let him get a word in edgewise.

C. S. Lewis used to say that when a person wakes up in the morning, all his cares, concerns, frustrations come at him like a pack of wild animals. So he needs to train himself to shove them all back, shut them out as best he can, and try to listen to the one voice that can give him the real answer to effective living or how to walk a bit taller in the world. It is not easy to shut out those cares, concerns, sounds, and distractions, but we can discipline ourselves to do so.

When the coming and going of many people got too much for the disciples, Jesus told them, "Come with me, by yourselves, to some lonely place, where you can rest quietly." Christ's own life sets a pattern for silence. We can see at a glance what it was like in the first chapter of the Gospel of Mark. Up before dawn, Jesus goes off by himself to pray, to be silent, to listen. Then he goes out into the world to be anything but silent! He preaches to the people who are eager to hear him, and he heals a leper. Withdrawal, then advancing to speak, then off to one side to do an act of kindness was the pattern.

Time and time again, when the disciples got keyed up, when things seemed to be going well and they wanted to press on, Jesus would say no. He would make them withdraw with him for rest, silence, listening, a recharging of the spiritual batteries. He knew well how draining their ministry could be. "Come with me, by yourselves, to some lonely place where you can rest quietly," Jesus said to them, because, as Mark tells us, "They had no leisure even to eat, so many were coming and going."

Church people can often earn good marks for their proclamations, pronouncements, or simple acts of kindness for their fellow-men, but most of us fall down when it comes to the area Jesus put first: withdrawal to be still, to pray, to listen, to prepare ourselves.

Making constructive use of silence does not mean we have to go off to some mountain peak or desert island. We may learn to talk like the woman in a tenement who said, "When I want solitude, I just throw my apron over my head. That's all the solitude I get, but it works!" It is attitude that matters, not geography. There are times when we think the answer to our frustrations may be to move to a new town, buy a new house, change jobs or careers. We may even make a move or two, but what happens? We find the same problems and the same frustrations. A change of scene was not the answer after all.

This lesson reminds me of the story of an old innkeeper in Southern France the day two neighbors came to see him. Both neighbors were moving away. One was obviously delighted to be going: he hated the town. The other neighbor was broken-hearted about leaving: the town meant much to him and to his family.

"I'm glad I'm leaving," said the first man. "I never liked the people in this town."

"I'm sorry," said the innkeeper, "because you're going to find the same kind of people where you are going."

Along came the second neighbor. His attitude was quite the opposite. He said to the innkeeper, "I am really sad to have to leave this town. I love the people of this community. My wife and I have a host of friends here. We feel we have a kind of investment in people. We hate to have to move on."

"Don't worry," said the innkeeper, "because you're going to find the same kind of people where you are going."

The answer to frustrations may not be found in geography but in a state of mind and in the realm of the spirit, in latching on to those qualities Christ came to teach us: faith, trust, quiet, dependence on that strength beyond self which can come only from God.

But how can you and I best go about making constructive use of silence in our own efforts toward spiritual growth? I cannot suggest what may work best for you, but I can throw out a few suggestions I know others have found work for them and add a few of my own as springboards for still better ideas you may be able to develop on your own.

A Rutgers University professor has taught me that it is important, not only to be free of interruptions (if only for a few minutes), but also to be free of the fear of them. Who has not had the experience of sitting in a room with a telephone you just knew would ring—and, sure enough, it did!

I usually begin by reading the psalm for the day. Sometimes it's way over my head, and I get nothing from it. At other times a verse or two or maybe a whole psalm will "sing" to me. No matter. Just beginning with the psalm seems to help set the tone for what follows.

Next I read a short Bible passage, usually from a modern translation such as The New English Bible. Instead of haphazardly choosing a portion of Scripture, I find it useful to follow an orderly table like the lectionary in the front of the Prayer Book or some other outline. The American Bible Society publishes useful tables of lessons as do most denominations.

Then comes prayer itself, not just one kind of prayer but adoration, confession, thanksgiving, intercession, and petition. ACTIP helps one to remember these so-called five fingers of prayer. If one adds meditation to that list and rearranges the order, the word IMPACT will help call all six forms to mind.

This practice leads finally to those few minutes we have been considering in this chapter—those minutes devoted to silence, shutting out the world about us with its sounds and distractions, and just listening. Such moments of silence may be difficult to come by at first. They may take practice. At first we may not "hear" very much. But I believe God *may* speak to us in such moments or possibly speak to us later on in the day, precisely because we *have* consciously "tuned in" and honestly tried to let him get a word in earlier.

I have warned my family: when they see me go off by myself in the morning for a few moments of silence, they are not to think I have flipped my lid. I am just trying to make constructive use of silence. I am convinced doing so can help a person get on top of life instead of letting life get on top of him or her.

When we sing John Greenleaf Whittier's great hymn "Dear Lord and Father of Mankind," we sing the words, "Forgive our *foolish* ways." Actually, I believe the author originally wrote, "Forgive our *feverish* ways," which might come closer to speaking to us today. But in the third stanza we come upon words that encourage us in the constructive use of silence, with God's help, in our own efforts to grow:

> Drop thy still dews of quietness
>   Till all our strivings cease;
> Take from our souls the strain and stress
> And let our ordered lives confess
>   The beauty of thy peace.

A Prayer of Thanksgiving

Almighty God, Father of all mercies, we thank thee for all thou hast given, and for all thou hast forgiven us. We thank thee for thy hidden blessings and for those which in our negligence we have passed over; for every gift of nature or of grace; for the power of loving; for all thou hast yet in store for us; for everything, whether joy or sorrow, whereby thou art drawing us to thyself; through Jesus Christ our Lord. Amen.

—St. Paul's Cathedral, Boston

6

Saying Thanks

How can one become conscious of the presence of God and begin to build a deeper relationship with him? One good way to begin is by saying thanks.

The New Testament is shot through with reminders that the Christian wants to express thanks to God. But it is a sad fact that for most of us thanksgiving is one of the most neglected forms of prayer. It is sad because saying thanks to God takes us out of ourselves, helps us regain perspective, and helps us rearrange our priorities.

Remember the story of Jesus and the ten lepers? Ten were cured, but only one bothered to come back and say thanks. Theologians remind us that the one who came back entered into a living relationship with Christ that the others never knew, and that relationship began with little more than a simple thank you!

In Pittsburgh the other day, a woman asked me, "Why don't we get to sing 'Count your blessings, name them one by one'?"

I was tempted to say, "It's a dreadful hymn tune, but it's a good thought," because we would do well to catalogue our blessings more than we do.

The next day, I got to thinking about persons I know who have taught me something about counting my blessings and giving thanks. One was a man I met at a dinner party in Lawrenceville, New Jersey. He said, "When I say thanks, I've got to be specific. I have to thank God for *this* particular friendship or *that* specific opportunity. If I thank God for just everything, know what happens? I end up feeling I haven't really thanked him for anything. I find I have to be specific."

The second person who has taught me something about thanksgiving is a father in New York who says, "I don't just thank God for tangible things. I thank him for intangibles, too: the trust of a little child or a good night's sleep or the good opinion of my colleagues at the office. These are intangibles all right, but they are blessings you can't measure or put price tags on." And that person is the parent of two daughters who contracted a rare disease thirty years ago, stopped growing, and are still alive today.

The third person who has taught me something about thanksgiving is in the office equipment business. He told me, "Sometimes I find it helpful even to thank God for problems. I may say, 'God, you have given me this situation. What would you have me do about it?' You know what happens? Sometimes the situation will be changed or I'll somehow seem to get strength to cope. Often I seem to be changed a bit in the process."

At church last Sunday, I paid special attention to the words of the Prayer of General Thanksgiving. We said again, as so often before, that we thanked God above all for his inestimable love "in the redemption of the world by our Lord Jesus Christ; for the means of grace and for the hope of glory." Then we went on to say, "Give us that due sense of all thy mercies, that our hearts may be unfeignedly thankful; and that we show forth thy praise, not only with our lips, but in our lives. . . ."

I thought how true it was that the "due sense" of all his mercies can cause a person to come back at awkward situations with the unexpected finer response. Sometimes it can cause us to "sound off" when we might be expected to keep still or to keep still when we might be expected to sound off.

For some, faith acts as a kind of shock absorber.

It can sensitize a person to somebody else's needs, needs no one else has recognized. Faith may enable a person to see in someone else something of what Christ sees in that person, to love the seemingly unlovable and to forgive the seemingly unforgivable. Faith can give a person staying power.

Out in Arizona the nine-year-old daughter of a friend of mine went to church school one Sunday when the teacher asked, "What would you do if Jesus were to appear in this classroom?"

One boy put up his hand and said, "I guess I'd ask to see the nail prints in his hands or the sword wound in his side."

My friend's little girl said, "Oh, I don't think I'd do that. I suppose I'd just say thank you for all he has done for us."

If we can honestly learn to thank God for all our blessings, not holding them possessively to ourselves but offering them to him to use, we can make a real start at spiritual growth.

A Prayer for Forgiveness

Be gracious to me, O God, in thy true love; in the fulness of thy mercy blot out my misdeeds. Wash away my guilt and cleanse me from my sin. Create a pure heart in me, O God, and give me a new and steadfast spirit; do not drive me from thy presence or take thy Holy Spirit from me; revive in me the joy of thy deliverance and grant me a willing spirit to uphold me. Amen.

—Psalm 51:1, 2, 10-12 (NEB)

7

Saying You're Sorry

THE STORY IS told of a bum who stumbled into an Episcopal church just as the congregation was saying the prayer of general confession. He heard the congregation say, "We have left undone those things which we ought to have done, and we have done those things which we ought not to have done, and there is no health in us." Plunking himself down in the nearest pew, he sighed, "Obviously, this is my crowd!"

I tell this story, not to be irreverent about a great prayer, but to suggest how much that prayer strikes home. Most of us are sorry about things we have done or left undone. No doubt we all experience times when we wish we could wipe the slate clean and start over. We wish that we could somehow find the road home, the joy of reconciliation with God the Father, instead of feeling a gnawing sense that our life is not all we hoped it might be, a stinging realization that life is incomplete.

Some years ago, I saw Jean-Louis Forain's etching of the Prodigal Son which shows the boy kneeling before his father. (It is the frontispiece of this book.) I found it haunting. It moved me so much that I asked a museum to make a photocopy of it. The shoulders of the father as he leans toward his son wonderfully suggest the love and forgiveness he must have felt as he first heard his son say, "Father, I am sorry."

The Prodigal Son had taken off, gone to a far-off country, and virtually thrown away his life. When he hit bottom, he decided to return home and ask his father to take him back. He practiced over and over again what he could say to his father when he first saw him. He would offer no excuses, admit everything. You know the rest: how his father spotted the boy afar off and rushed out to greet him; the boy dropped to his knees. Before he could deliver half his rehearsed speech, his father flung his arms about the boy and embraced him.

The Parable of the Prodigal Son reminds us that no matter what we have ever done or said, no matter how mixed-up or messy our lives may be, our heavenly Father will still take us back, be our friend, and stay with us forever. God can restore the broken relationship as though it had never been broken at all. The gospel of Jesus Christ is the good news of a second chance. The road home to reconciliation begins when one says, "Father, I am sorry."

"*We have left undone those things which we ought to have done.*" When I hear those words, they remind me of a letter I received last spring from a friend of mine who is very ill and living, as he said, "on borrowed time." He said, "Lee, I am writing you to square accounts and set the record straight. For some years I have had the feeling you blamed me for something that happened to you that once hurt you deeply. I was not responsible, and I wanted to set the record straight by telling you so." When I read that letter, I said to myself, I wonder what I would do if I felt I were living on borrowed time. What would I do to get my house in order? I suppose I would go to my checkbook first, maybe write some letters I had put off writing. I might make a few phone calls or go see certain people I have long intended to go see or call. Why is it that we seem to wait until time is running out before we take care of unfinished business? In trying to find the way home,

I suppose we want to say, "Father, I am sorry," in specific terms for this or that opportunity I let slip by or maybe something I left unsaid.

"We have done those things which we ought not to have done." When I read those words, I remind myself I may not be guilty of headline crimes, but I may very well be guilty of a lot of things that tend to be invisible to me. You know what I mean—times I have allowed myself to be self-satisfied, depressed, ill-tempered, ungrateful. Or times when I have made decisions too much on the basis of the external world about me rather than on the basis of that inner voice or prompting of the Holy Spirit. Perhaps I have gone so far as to tell myself, "Lee, forget it! You're no worse than anybody else. Everyone is doing this or that." Or those times when I have failed really to forgive others. To find the road home, we want to say, "Father, I am sorry" and say it honestly and in specific terms, perhaps mentioning some unkind word we let slip out yesterday or some self-indulgence we allowed ourselves today.

Second, to find the road home, we may want to correct things or make amends where possible for what we have done or left undone. The other day a dentist friend of mine confronted a seventeen-year-old boy who had willfully damaged a table in the waiting room by carving his initials in the top.

"What are you going to do about it?" the dentist asked.

It was obvious the boy planned to do nothing.

"Guess I'll have to call your mother," said my friend.

"She wouldn't talk to you!" said the boy. (My friend had no thought of calling the boy's mother. He didn't show anger, he managed to keep his cool.)

Next day, the boy returned, saying, "Doctor, I owe you an apology. I was wrong. I am sorry. Tell you what I'd like to do about it. I can sandpaper down the table and refinish it for you. As a matter of fact, I have some sandpaper here in my pocket."

"No, I just wanted to hear you say you were sorry. That was all. The fact that you have the sandpaper in your pocket shows you really mean what you said."

Christ made it clear that we are going to want to "forgive those who trespass against us," those who have done or wished us evil. "If you forgive men their trespasses, your heavenly Father will also forgive you."

I have a talented young friend down south. When he was in high school, he found he had a real gift for working with young people and devoted long hours to volunteer work among ghetto-area teen-agers there.

71

When he went on to Harvard, he had not been in Cambridge more than a few weeks when a gang stabbed him. The knife missed killing him by inches. A few days later, his rector reached him by phone. Robert was still on the critical list. The rector asked him how he was. Robert was not bitter, just grateful to be alive.

"Would you do something for me?" he asked. "Would you see to it that you have prayers at all services next week for the breaking down of hatred and violence in our country?" That was how much Robert understood the way Christian forgiveness works!

It has helped me to hear the idea of forgiving others explained the way a Washington pastor once illustrated it to a woman who wanted to understand the meaning of Christian forgiveness in her own life. He told her, "Our wrong-doings cut us off from other human beings. God reaches down to hold my hand. With my other hand, I reach out to touch the lives of fellow human beings. Only as both connections are made can the power flow. And sin will break the connection every time. Perhaps that is why our Lord was specific in warning us that if we really want forgiveness ourselves, we are going to want to forgive others."

Imagine yourself as the Prodigal Son. You fall to

your knees and say, "Father, I am sorry." The words are hardly on your lips when you feel your father's arms around you and the joy and forgiveness they express. You feel his love because the father was watching the road for you every bit as much as you were watching the road ahead of you for the first glimpse of home—and that father coming toward you.

No matter what we have ever said or done, no matter how mixed up or messy our lives may be, the return home is still possible. Our heavenly Father will take us back, be our friend, and stay with us forever. God can restore our broken relationship with him as though it had never been broken. The gospel of Jesus Christ is still good news of a second chance. And, as with the Prodigal Son, it all begins when we say, "Father, I am sorry."

A Prayer for Guidance

O God, by whom the meek are guided in judgment, and light riseth up in darkness for the godly; grant us, in all our doubts and uncertainties, the grace to ask what thou wouldst have us to do, that the Spirit of Wisdom may save us from all false choices, and that in thy light we may see light, and in thy straight path may not stumble; through Jesus Christ our Lord. Amen.

—William Bright
(1824-1901)

A Prayer for Diligence

O God, who hast commanded that no one should be idle, give us grace to employ all our talents and faculties in the service appointed to us; that whatsoever our land findeth to do, we may do it with all our might; through Jesus Christ our Lord. Amen.

—James Martineau
(1805-1900)

8

What Have We
to Offer?

EVER NOTICE HOW often we waste time bemoaning our lack of this or that instead of making full use of what we have?

The pop writer bemoans the fact that he is not up to composing for the New York Philharmonic. The superb cartoonist, whose weekly drawings hit home in papers across the country, bemoans the fact that he will never be able to paint a picture that will land in the National Gallery. The housewife, who can make a first-rate gourmet soup, bemoans the fact that the poetry she writes is only second-rate.

All of us are different. Just as our fingerprints differ, each of us is different in countless other ways from anyone who ever lived—even within our own families. IQ tests and aptitude tests show how different we are. So, in other ways, do the monthly statements from the bank. But, as one advertising executive told colleagues at the office, "Isn't it great that everybody is not alike, or they'd all want to be married to my wife!"

Part of any Christian's vocation is to try to recognize what God has given him or her and make the most of it, hopefully coming ever closer to what may be God's highest hopes for that life. The Parable of the Talents is not the story of eight coins or talents; it is the story of three men and what they did with what had been given them. It is an age-old story that has given the adjective *talented* to the English language. You remember how the master became furious with the third man who had only buried in the ground the one talent he had. Outraged, the master said, "Why did you not put it in the bank where it would at least have earned interest?"

To make the most of what God has given us—resources, talent, energy, time—we have to dig down deep to learn a bit more about ourselves and who we are. Instead of losing ourselves in evasive overbusiness, we need to make more of the job of getting to know who we are. I am not suggesting what Baron von Hügel called "a spiritual flea hunt." Nor do I think we should soak in a kind of "introspective bath." I *am* suggesting that we may want to analyze what makes us tick, our strengths and weaknesses, more than we do, and ask Christ's help in approaching our true potential.

In his book *A Way to Live, A Way to Pray*, author John Coburn says that when he was head of a theological seminary and served on its admissions committee, he used to make a point of asking each candidate what he felt was his greatest strength as a human being and what he considered his greatest weakness. Nine times out of ten, he said, "the strength the person named was also identified as the source of weakness." Strangely enough, each person's strength and his weakness seemed somehow to be interrelated.

For instance, he said, one candidate might say, "I am very patient with people. That is my greatest asset. My greatest weakness is that I have difficulty standing up to people even when I know they are wrong."

Another person might tell him that administrative ability seemed to be his greatest asset, the capacity to get things done. Then the candidate might feel he had to admit, "But my greatest disability as a human being is that I can be pretty ruthless if people get in my way."

What seems to be your greatest strength as a human being or your greatest weakness? Are the two interrelated? How, with God's help, do you think you could use what he has given you to invest in the lives of others?

Most of us tend to tell ourselves, "I haven't much to offer. I haven't any influence. How on earth could God ever use a person like me?"

Paul was addressing the little church in Corinth, but he might well have been speaking to you and me today when he wrote, "Not many wise men after the flesh, not many mighty, not many noble are called: But God hath chosen the foolish things of the world to confound the wise; and God hath chosen the weak things of the world to confound the things which are mighty" (1 Cor. 1:26–27).

History is full of examples of what just one person can do. One vote brought the Third French Republic into being. One electoral vote put Rutherford B. Hayes in the White House. One vote saved the Selective Service Act just a few weeks before Pearl Harbor in 1941. And I have seen one man write a letter to an acquaintance he hardly knew about eighty-three political prisoners he had never met but who he understood were being held illegally in an Italian prison. That single letter proved to be responsible for freeing eighty-two of the prisoners within a month and has always reminded me of what one individual can do!

If you think your life doesn't count for much, that you have little or no potential influence, try this experiment. Count the number of people you talk to in a given day, from the time you get out of bed in the morning until you go back to bed again at night—the elevator operator, the bus driver, the girl at the supermarket check-out counter, the person who works down the hall whose name you've never bothered to learn, the people you talk to on the phone, the people to whom you write letters. Count them all, and see if you are not astonished at the number of lives you touch in a single day.

If we are trying to dig deep and really get to know ourselves, if we honestly want God's help in approaching our true potential, prayer may help us begin to see differently those whom we meet each day. If you are aware that some neighbor is tied up in knots and in need of human contact it could be that God has made you conscious of that person's need because he hopes you will do something about it. It may mean reaching out to that neighbor in some such simple way as listening to that person talk about his or her problems over a cup of coffee. I happen to believe God may put your name or mine on certain opportunities in the hope that we will be on the lookout for them and—with his help —follow through.

A close friend of mine, Kenneth Chorley, was very much involved in the restoration of Colonial Williamsburg. More than once he told me, "I am not an artist, archaeologist, engineer, or historian. Woe is me if I ever pretend to be what I'm not! Once I have found the artists, archaeologists, and so on, to work for us, my job is to try to be a catalyst who helps these various experts to work effectively together. You know, it's sometimes important to recognize what you cannot do before you can really zero in on the area where you can contribute most."

Back in the 1960s I knew a bishop who became disturbed that one of the priests in his diocese seemed to be neglecting some of his parish duties. When the bishop looked into the situation, he discovered the priest was devoting a good share of his time to courtroom work, helping young people in trouble. Apparently the priest had such a gift for that kind of work that the bishop—instead of reprimanding him—found him extra help for his parish so that he could be free to continue this special work for which he had such a gift.

You watch a man who has the gift of insight stand up at a town meeting that seems hopelessly deadlocked. He uses that gift of insight to show both factions where they are actually in agreement and where their principal differences could be eliminated. If he did not use that God-given gift of insight, chances are he would lose it.

Or you watch a woman who has discovered she has a talent for listening. She seems to have a gift for helping patients at a sanitarium just by listening. She seems able to sit at a bedside and radiate concern and reassurance to a depressed patient simply by sitting and listening. She radiates a kind of strength that may be as helpful at times as the prescription on that patient's bedside table. If she did not listen but became instead a chatterbox, her special gift might indeed be altogether lost.

As you and I reexamine the landscape of our lives and try to recognize opportunities to invest in the lives of others what God has given to us, we will do well to remember that we do not have to go it alone. Christianity is not a do-it-yourself proposition. Jesus promised us his help, himself, in approaching our true potential, but there were strings attached! The gift was offered on condition we would accept him on *his* terms. Chances are, he has higher hopes for our lives than we do.

Our experience can be a little like that of the first man in the parable whose five talents became ten. God can multiply our effectiveness many times over, a little like the rich man I once knew. When he learned that his poor friends had made a donation to some charity—a donation they could ill afford to make—he would anonymously make an additional gift four times as large, unbeknownst to those friends, in their name, not his own.

We may also discover that we are not being called to do more church work, important as that may be, or to do work that is completely new. The call may be to stay where we already are and do what we are already doing but to do it in a new spirit because we have caught something of the contagion of Christ. The old Latin motto says, *Non novus sed nove,* not new things but old things seen or done in a new way.

If Paul were writing to Americans today, he might picture the Christian teacher finding a ministry in helping young people to grow intellectually and as persons, the Christian manufacturer determined that his product be everything his ads claim it to be, the Christian wife concerned most about her husband's happiness and that of her children, and her husband concerned not only with their happiness but also with his wife's chance to realize everything in life she potentially can be.

Paul reminded the church at Corinth, "There

are varieties of gifts, but the same Spirit. There are varieties of service, but the same Lord. There are many forms of work, but all of them, in all men, are the work of the same God. In each of us the Spirit is manifested in one particular way, for some useful purpose. . . . But all these gifts are the work of one and the same Spirit, distributing them separately to each individual at will" (1 Cor. 12:4-8, 11, NEB).

God has given each of us some talent, but he does not care if it makes you or me famous. All he cares about is that we use what he has lent us as best we can so that the world is the better for it. As Paul wrote to Timothy, we are to stir up what God has lent us and not deprive him of it if someday we are to hear his voice say, "Well done, good and faithful servant."

A Prayer of Dedication

Take and receive, O Lord, my entire liberty, my understanding, my memory, and my entire will. All that I am, all that I have thou hast given me, and I give them back to thee to be disposed of according to thy good pleasure. Give me only thy grace and thy love. With thee am I rich enough. Nor do I ask for aught besides; through Jesus Christ our Lord. Amen.

—St. Ignatius Loyola
(1491-1556)

9

Fulfilling Our Ministry

I ALMOST BEGAN a talk at church the other day by pulling a nasty trick on the congregation. I thought of asking for a show of hands of all the ministers present. Had I done that, you know what would have happened. The clergy would have put up their hands. The rest of us lay men and women would not have moved a muscle.

But isn't that all wrong? Didn't Christ call all of us—clergy and laity alike—to be his ministers, his ambassadors or representatives where we work and where we live? Sure, our clergy have an important special function to perform within the church, but hasn't our Lord called everyone of us who profess and call ourselves Christians to share in his church's ministry to the world? It seems to me the spirit of his words was directed at all of us when he said, ". . . and you will bear witness for me in Jerusalem and all over Judaea and Samaria and away to the ends of the earth."

The idea that we are all ministers or ambassadors can put us off a bit. You may say, "I'm not about to stand up and give sermons in the parking lot or lead hymn-sings by the water cooler during a coffee break at the office." I'm sure you won't, but being Christ's representatives may call us to go to bat for him more often in a lot of other ways—such as how we see human beings represented in a balance sheet or affected by this or that personnel policy change, how we come back at someone else's anger, how willing we may be to listen to tiresome complaints from someone's sickbed, how we bounce back from difficult reverses, what kind of staying power we maintain in seeing a worthy program through to completion.

Our ministry may call us, not to give a speech, but, more importantly, to say a word or two to one upset person in the company cafeteria. Our ministry may call us to radiate something of Christ's spirit, not just by saying or doing anything, but by being there when we're needed. Often, there's a great ministry in just being physically present somewhere, in putting your arms about someone to let that person know you care.

Legend tells that after Jesus' ascension he was met at the gate of heaven by an archangel who said, "You chose your disciples and told them to go out to others, and so on, until ultimately all the world was won. Well, suppose that doesn't happen? Suppose they don't follow through. What then?"

Jesus replied simply, "I have no other plan."

How can we possibly measure up? Perhaps we should begin by following the example of Jesus and how he ordered his own life. As I see it, the Gospels show at least three recurrent themes we may find helpful in discovering our ministry.

First, Jesus withdrew regularly from the distractions of the world to prepare himself to meet it. Near Capernaum he went off by himself to pray first thing in the morning. In Galilee he sent the people away so that he could be alone to pray. And he saw to it that his disciples withdrew as well.

I know a man who depends on an alarm clock to wake him up for a few minutes of prayer before the household gets going and he has to go off to work. And I know a housewife who sees to it she doesn't forget to pray. She tapes prayers or names of people she wants to remember to the refrigerator door. She's a dear, sweet soul, and you should see the refrigerator!

Each of us leads his or her own life. You will want to follow the plan that works best for you, but here's hoping we will want to make it our practice to withdraw perhaps more than we have to date.

Second, Jesus seems to have focused most of his attention on other people in close-ups—not distance shots taken with a wide-angle lens. Oh, sure we read of his preaching to crowds on a hillside or from a boat or feeding great hordes of people at times, but most of the Gospel narratives tell us about his person-to-person encounters. He coaxed little Zacchaeus down from a tree, met with Nicodemus after dark, gave the sisters Mary and Martha a lesson in priorities, warned the rich young ruler about loving his wealth too much. He picked a little child up in his lap and sympathized with the sisters of Lazarus when he learned of their brother's death.

Jesus focused his life in close-ups in much the way that a great pastor will do today. I think of the famous rector of a big city parish who wasn't much of a preacher, but what a pastor! I remember the time a Girl Scout official came to call on him, raising funds. She was very articulate and went into a long, very professional spiel. The rector took out his checkbook, said he'd be glad to help. Then he looked over at that woman who had spoken so articulately about her Girl Scout programs. "But tell me about yourself, child," he said. With this the woman burst into floods of tears—tears that had been building up during months of loneliness. Here was someone actually caring about her life.

Jesus focused his life in close-ups. Maybe our ministry should be a centered-down person-to-person program that does not lose sight of the individuals God may have put close to you and me for a reason!

Third, Jesus had a preternatural gift for reading people right and dealing, not just with the external symptoms that troubled them, but with the root causes. As the Scripture says, "The Lord does not see as man sees; men judge by appearances but the Lord judges by the heart" (1 Sam. 16:7, NEB).

You never read about Jesus asking someone, "What's so-and-so like?" He had a gift for reading people accurately. Look at the way he spoke to the woman at the well: "Go home, call your husband, and come back."

"I have no husband," said she.

"You are right," said Jesus looking directly at her. "You have no husband. You've had five!"

Look at Jesus near the pool where he sees a man who's been a cripple thirty-eight years. He doesn't cure the man straight off. He first asks, "Do you want to recover?" Deep down sometimes there are those who don't want to be cured, sick people who enjoy the attention misery brings them. Jesus wanted the man to admit he wanted to get well.

When Jesus set about curing a sick person, he looked beyond external symptoms. When the people brought a paralytic to him, he didn't first say, "Stand up and walk." He first said, "Your sins are forgiven." Only later did he tell the man, "Stand up and walk." No doubt at first the man was surprised and thought, "What's this all about?"

A skin doctor today sees a housewife distressed about a rash on her face. "What's troubling you?" he may ask before prescribing medication, and he learns the root cause—an alcoholic husband who refuses to face his problem and seek help.

The other day a delivery man parked in an inconvenient spot on the street in front of our neighbor's house. It was hard for cars to pass. I found myself getting annoyed when it suddenly occurred to me: the poor man has multiple sclerosis. It is hard for him to get around. It's a miracle at times he can work at all. No wonder he parks as close to each house as he possibly can. It made me realize again how important it is to look beyond what people do, lest we misjudge them.

I know a clergyman whose office is on the third floor of a building with no elevator. When he hears a person clumping up the stairs to see him, he says, "I try to remember to pray, 'Lord help me to read this person right.' I do that, and I know it helps."

When we come up against other people's actions or reactions we do not understand, an aloofness perhaps, or unexplainable short temper, or whatever, maybe we'd do well to pray, "Lord, what's behind that attitude? Help me to read this person right, and help me to help."

Our Lord did indeed call all of us, clergy and laity alike, to be his ministers or representatives. We are not wonderful if we accept opportunities to answer that call; we are perhaps answerable if we don't. Jesus promised us his help, and we have his example to guide us—the way he made it a practice to withdraw, the way he focused his life in close-ups, and the way he tried to see root causes behind the superficial symptoms.

In *The Story of Jesus,* Theodore Parker Ferris suggests our Lord says in effect to you and me today, "Do this in remembrance of me. Do in your own imperfect and inadequate way the thing that I did. Let the glory shine through the breakage, that people may pick up the broken pieces of their lives and lead better lives because of you."

Our Lord may not count on you and me to do much about Judaea or Samaria these days, but isn't he counting on us to do our part where we work and live in New York or Westchester County or Connecticut, in New Jersey or California or wherever, to

91

show the world that he is in us and we in him? We will show that we are his by what we do, by what we say, and, above all, most importantly, by what we are and what Christ knows us to be . . . "unto whom all hearts are open, all desires known, and from whom no secrets [even yours and mine] are hid."

A Prayer for Peace

O God, who only makest us to dwell in safety, open my eyes to see myself as others see me, and to see others as Thou seest them. Help me to love those I do not like and to be of good will toward those I meet daily: Only then dare I pray for the peace of the world in the name of the Prince of Peace, Jesus Christ our Saviour. Amen.

—Wilburn C. Campbell

10

Becoming a Peacemaker

A WHILE BACK Mary Mason, a schoolteacher in Princeton where I live, tried her hand at writing a book of Bible stories and teachings for little children. To make sure she was getting through to her young age-group, Miss Mason tape-recorded the reactions of children in one of her classes. Their reactions were wonderful!

The children were convinced the Israelites had no mommies and daddies because the Bible talked only about the children of Israel. And the boys and girls were convinced that everybody at the time of the first Christmas must have gone to Bethlehem in taxis because the children did not understand the meaning of the word *taxes*. (Ah, to be a child again just for one day!) When Miss Mason asked the chil-

dren about peacemakers, the children just talked
about shoemakers—the only *makers* they knew.
Peacemakers, builders for peace—who were they?

I guess it's true; we don't use the word *peacemaker* very much because too few of us qualify!
And yet aren't all of us who profess and call ourselves Christians, who have promised to follow the
Prince of Peace—aren't we called to be peacemakers, catalysts, reconcilers? To use the jargon of
our day, "It's all a part of the deal!"

When I first went into public relations work some
years ago, one of the first lessons I learned was that
just about everything and everybody is connected.
And I learned, too, that the creative person is not
necessarily the person who can write sonnets or
compose a symphony. He or she may be the kind of
person who sees relationships in the seemingly un-
related, how this over here may be related to that,
how a principle at work in this field might successfully be borrowed and applied in quite another field
over there. Such a person somehow sees relationships others fail to see. He or she seems to have a
different kind of vision. Remembering that everybody is somehow connected and cultivating a different kind of vision may be helpful ideas for a
business executive to bear in mind. They may be

helpful ideas for the would-be peacemaker to bear in mind as well.

We all know how easy, cozy, and comfortable it can be to try to be catalysts or peacemakers at home where the atmosphere is familiar and congenial. I dare say it is not always so easy, cozy, and comfortable out in the harsh, larger world where the barriers may go up and one comes face to face with the unfamiliar and the sometimes hostile.

I suppose it can be a common temptation for most of us to let our thoughts of peacemaking drift toward something rather distant or remote, to problems we know we cannot do much about. It is a temptation to let our thoughts drift far away rather than concern ourselves with more immediate tensions closer to home. It is far easier, heaven knows, to talk in vague terms about Southeast Asia or the oil crisis in the Near East than to go on a walk through the slums of our own city or to visit a nearby prison to learn about opportunities to help there.

One day in World War II when I was working for an army chaplain, a middle-aged sergeant, down in the dumps, came to see my boss. It was clear the sergeant had a bad case of self-pity. He was feeling very sorry for himself. Looking at him, the chaplain asked, "You know what's wrong? You're living in too small a world, a little circle where you're the one right smack in the center. You're not likely to find much happiness, I'm afraid, until that circle gets a bit larger and you put someone else in the center!"

All of us live in a series of concentric circles, each a bit bigger than the other. I suppose all of us live in at least ten circles. There's the smallest one, the family circle, then the neighborhood (that's a bit larger), the town, the state, the nation, the world, or the office, the larger circle of our profession or business, our political party, our church, and so on. And isn't the Christian called to be something of a peacemaker in all those various circles? Edmund Burke once said, "All that is necessary for the forces of evil to win in the world is for enough good men [or women] to do nothing."

We are called to serve all kinds of people, not just those close to us or congenial. The Christian is called to be a peacemaker and serve, not just the friendly, but the hostile as well, the attractive and the unattractive, rich and poor, the talented and the untalented. He is called to serve all.

In the air force these days the current expression is "to stay loose." It would be well, I suppose, for most of us to stay loose more often than we do, more open to new opportunities, new people, new dimensions in living. A friend of mine says, "To be open is simply to be more aware on deeper and deeper levels of what exists in your total life situation and in yourself."

"Blessed are the peacemakers; for they shall be called the children of God." In the ten or so concentric circles of your life, do you see here and there a place where you might be more of a peacemaker than you have been to date?

When I look about me at people I consider catalysts or peacemakers, I see friends directly or indirectly helping the sick in my community, others working quite hard to see some laws made more just, others devoting themselves to breaking down tensions between certain groups they understand. I see their work and become acutely conscious of the many forms building for peace can take.

The word *peacemaker* calls to my mind a number of people. For instance, I remember a friend of mine in the dry goods business. He found himself in a deadlocked strike situation. I well recall the day he and the labor union head bowed their heads in a silent prayer that both men later said "at least conditioned the atmosphere" of their tense meeting room.

I remember Wilburn Campbell, a bishop friend of mine, meeting with a group of legislators. "I am

not trying to put the church into politics," he said
with a twinkle. "I'm just trying to put Christ into
the politicians."

I recall reading about Woodrow Wilson sounding
off at Versailles after World War I about his hopes
for the future. Clemenceau stood it as long as he
could, then banged his hand down on the table.
"But Mr. Wilson, Mr. Wilson," he said, *"you're* talking like Jesus Christ!"

Closer to home, I think of the slum area teen-
ager in lower Manhattan who decided to try to put
an end to gang warfare in his neighborhood by
forming a peace council. It would be hard to forget
him because he began to recruit people for this
council by first going to the gang that had murdered
his own brother.

I think of a group of lay men and women who
worked hard after World War II to get a meditation room set aside for the use of delegates to the
UN. "It will take an archangel to get it," Ralph
Bunche told those laymen, "but I wish you well in
your efforts!" Well, the room did not become a real-
ity overnight. It took months and lots of hard work,
but the efforts of those dedicated laymen paid off.
When it became evident to the powers that be at the
UN that here were concerned laymen who had no
axe to grind, who were interested only in the good

that could be done, not personal credit, who were even content to remain anonymous, doors began to open and the opposition and red tape began to disappear.

As builders for peace, how well do you and I measure up? I suppose most of us are deeply conscious of the way in which we tend to spread ourselves too thin. We take on too much and fail to do what we do in depth. When we really take stock, we become conscious that we need a new vision and a new strength. We come to feel we need spiritual transplants, eyes to see in others something of what Christ sees in them or hearts to help us put ourselves in the shoes of other people we'd like to reach and help. And here's where we come around again to recognize our basic need to find God through prayer.

Someone once asked the late William Temple why he believed in prayer. He said, "Because when I pray, coincidences happen; when I stop, they stop!"

In prayer you and I take our needs, our problems, the worries that are eating us, to God and wait for him to give us a new vision and a new strength. The true measure of what our life adds up to is not so much determined by what we do as by what we let God do through us when we "let go and let God,"

101

when we let him have his way with us. This means putting Christ at the center of those concentric circles.

"These all belong together," John Coburn writes, "Christ in the inner self, love in personal relationships, and justice between groups within the nation and between nations." There is a famous old saying that justice is "love working at long range."

Prayer can be hard work. We will have our ups and downs, our frustrations. We may not see results overnight. Waiting and listening can be important parts. We shall need ESP—expectancy, sensitivity, persistence. It will take all of this to answer the call to become peacemakers or children of God in our day.

Back in 1961 on Whitsunday or Pentecost, the late Dag Hammarskjöld wrote in his diary about his own experience in answering such a call. "I don't know Who—or What—put the question. I don't even remember answering. But at some moment I did answer *yes* to Someone—or Something—and from that hour I was certain that existence is meaningful and that therefore, my life in self-surrender had a goal."

May something akin to the experience of Dag Hammarskjöld be ours in days to come as you and I ask God to guide our feet into the way of peace.

A Prayer for Self-Forgetful Service

Teach us, good Lord, to serve thee as thou deservest: to give and not to count the cost; to fight and not to heed the wounds; To toil and not to seek for rest; To labor and not to ask for any reward Save that of knowing that we do thy will; through Jesus Christ our Lord. Amen.

—St. Ignatius Loyola
(1491-1556)

11

Giving Tells a Lot about You

GIVING TELLS A LOT about a person, about his or her heart and faith. What we give of time, talent, resources, indeed of ourselves, may show us much about the depth of our religious convictions and about where our hearts really lie.

When I think of my own giving, I realize how far short it often falls measured in terms of heart and sacrifice. I may send a token gift sometimes to this or that cause just to get the volunteer solicitor off my back. I may lend my name to a charity letterhead but do little or nothing to involve myself in that cause. Or my wife and I may give to the home for the aged that old sofa we really wanted to get rid of anyway. Not much heart and sacrifice back of that giving, is there?

And yet I look about me at what others give. Five orphans in Indiana gave stones they had collected on walks to and from school—worthless stones but treasures to those children. Day after day I look at a stuffed owl in my music studio. That owl was a present to me from the blind girl who made it, a girl who has never, of course, seen an owl in her life. There was heart back of that gift of the owl. There was heart back of those stones.

It is important to give of one's material resources, but it is also important to give of one's skills. After World War II, I had the privilege of getting to know Dame Myra Hess, the great pianist. During the London blitz, at considerable risk, she had played the piano every day at noon to lift the spirits of Londoners who came regularly to hear her. A hairdresser I know gives free appointments to mental patients at a neuropsychiatric hospital. "It's not much," she may tell you, "but it's what I do best, and I know it does something for those people to feel they look their best."

Some people cannot give great gifts of material things or money. Some may have only limited skills or talent to share. But isn't it true that all of us can periodically give the gift of time?

This came home to me when a forty-year-old widow, living alone in Nebraska, was stricken with a crippling stroke. When doctors had done all they could, thirty-one friends—one for each day of the month—made a pact, unbeknownst to her, that each would be in touch on a particular day every month to let her know someone cared. It might mean a phone call, taking her out for a drive, sending her a card or letter. It might be something small, but it would tell Alice she was remembered. She would know she was not forgotten or as alone as she may have felt at times.

Remember the time Jesus went to the Temple and sat on the porch, watching people come and go, dropping their offerings, large and small, into the great trumpet-mouthed chests? No doubt, he observed the proud givers as well as the shy ones. Suddenly, a certain widow came up, declared—as they all did—what she was about to drop in, then deposited two small coins, perhaps the cost of her next meal.

Jesus beckoned to the disciples and pointed to the widow. He said nothing until she had walked away, down the steps and out through the so-called Golden Gate. Then he said, "I tell you this poor widow has given more than any of the others. The others had more than enough to give. This widow had less than enough and yet gave all she had to live on."

Jesus may not see us drop in copper coins, but he may well watch us as we make our daily offerings— the letters we write, the phone calls we make, the time we spend with those who need us. He knows the heart or sacrifice behind what we do, and he is aware of what is left over. Is there more where this or that gift came from?

I heard of a big gift the other day made by a young couple just three hours after their little boy was run over and killed by a speeding automobile. Even though they were still in shock, the young parents called up the hospital to offer their son's eyes to the eye bank. And they later learned from two doctors—one in Ohio, the other in Vermont— that each had been able to transplant successfully one of those eyes to restore the sight of someone else. That couple made a great gift indeed, doubly great when one realizes the conditions under which they gave it.

Giving is a tricky business. Many of us may think of it just in terms of kindness, but—as some have said—kindness can be a substitute for love, something we offer to people whom we may not love, cannot love, or cannot be bothered to love. We use the phrase "cold as charity." Even philanthropy can be a cold proposition when it is not motivated by love. What a far cry from the poor widow dropping her coins into the Temple treasure chest!

I think of three different women working for our
hospital benefit in Princeton, New Jersey. They are
all good workers; they get things done. But how different their reasons for doing that work! One woman
seems to be involved because it is the "in" thing to
do and several friends she admires are involved in
it. Another woman seems to have involved herself
as an escape from the boredom and seeming futility
she feels at home. But, I suspect, the third woman
looks on that work as her personal thankoffering
to God for what that hospital has meant in times
of crisis to her own family. All three are doing
effective work, but what different hearts and motives
each brings to that work.

I think of people I have known who were inspired givers, who certainly knew the message of
the temple porch. A generous man from Brighton,
England, told me, "Sometimes I wish the gifts I
made were made at greater sacrifice." A lady in
Pittsburgh told me, "The greatest gifts one ever
makes are the ones the Internal Revenue Service
never hears about because they are not tax deduct-
ible!"

Many years ago I had the privilege of meeting
one of my great heroes, the late Albert Schweitzer,
musician, theologian, philosopher, and medical missionary, a man who turned his back on fame in many
fields to go to Africa because he felt God called

109

him to do so. He said something I have never forgotten: "When you get a chance to accept an opportunity to do some service to others and feel
called to do it and can say yes, accept that opportunity with no thought of heroism. Accept it with
sober enthusiasm, remembering the many other people in the world, willing and able, who may not be
in a position to do the same."

The next time we hesitate to give of ourselves because we think we have so little to give, the picture
of that widow on the Temple porch should remind
us that no matter how small our gift of time, talent,
and resources, it can become great in God's eyes if,
behind it, there is a sacrificial heart.

THE LITTLE GIFT THAT WAS A BIG ONE

No more the mighty Roman powers
Claim victories or great feats.
No more the massive Temple towers
Above Jerusalem's streets,
Yet still one hears
Across the years,
Distinct and quite apart
The clank of two small copper coins,
Gifts from a widow's heart.
—*Lee H. Bristol, Jr.*

110

A Prayer for Direction

O God, my boat is so small in a sea so large, strengthen and direct me into such channels as thou wouldest have me to go, and give me courage to reach past the edges of the familiar when it is thy will; through Jesus Christ our Lord. Amen.

12

Knowing Where You Are

EVER NOTICE HOW you can almost divide people into two categories—those who "play it safe," living in a kind of sailors' snug harbor, and those who have a "sense of where they are," who have the courage, as a college classmate of mine puts it, "to reach past the edges of the familiar"? Psychiatrists are forever getting patients to ask themselves, Who am I? But there is another important question we would do well to ask ourselves as we set out on a spiritual program.

When John McPhee once interviewed the basketball player Bill Bradley, he asked the man how he was able so often to shoot perfect baskets over his shoulder without looking. Bradley told him, "You develop a sense of where you are," a quality maybe all of us would do well to develop in life.

At Hamilton College, my blind classmate, Bob Russell, used to walk around the campus without a cane or a dog. He told us a sightless person learns to judge direction and distance by sound alone. "The sound of one's footsteps returns as an echo, having bounced from the tree," he said. The echo of his own footsteps, bouncing back from a tree or a wall, kept him from walking into some obstacle.

Bob and his family now have a summer place up on the St. Lawrence River where Bob likes nothing better than to go fishing by himself in a little boat. "So that I can go out by myself whenever I please," he says, "I have run a wire down to the edge of the dock, where I have mounted a large electric bell. Before I go down to the dock, I plug the line into an outlet in the house. A timing device permits the bell to ring only once every thirty seconds. If I row too far upwind to be able to hear the bell, I can fish without anxiety, because I can always drift downward and then I am again in touch with my base."

Bob maintains that everyone needs a base to go out from and needs the assurance that no matter how far he goes out, return is still possible. "Confidence that he has such a base," he says, "is all that gives him the courage to reach past the edges of the familiar. It may be what he knows, what he believes, the table round, or heaven itself. The river lies before me, a constant invitation, a constant challenge, and my bell is the thread of sound along which I return."

How does one develop that kind of perspective in life? How can we feel a sense of where we are in relationship to the world about us? By looking within ourselves, by looking outward at the world, and—most importantly—by looking upward to the author and finisher of our faith.

Looking within. The Greeks said, "Know thyself." Socrates warned that to live the unexamined life was not to live at all. And Dag Hammarskjöld pointed out that the journey inward to self-knowledge is the longest journey a person will make. But it is a journey each of us must make.

Throughout this journey, however, it is important not to take oneself too seriously. Laughing at yourself can do wonders in maintaining perspective. One educator I know says, "When I look at my face in the shaving mirror each morning, I often say, 'You fool!' If what I am doing with my life is really important, I cannot afford to take myself too seriously."

Looking outward. When we look beyond the little world of our own homes or our own jobs, we may become frustrated by the complexities. Seemingly insoluble problems lie "out there"—intergroup tensions, crime, scandal, international discord. But aren't there some areas where—with God's help— we can let others feel the "stubborn ounces of our weight"?

A survey of the religious concerns of workers in one industrial community uncovered the fact that even church-going workers said they prayed about their families, their health, their other off-the-job concerns, but seldom about what happened on the job in the office or factory. Somehow they failed to see life as all of one piece and their faith related to every area of it.

I once knew a man in Kansas City who used the morning newspaper as a beginning for his morning prayers. He saw the paper as a kind of prayer book and would literally pray about this or that bereaved family that had lost a relative in an automobile accident, the Texas town damaged in a storm, that deadlocked strike situation in Michigan. This concern about the world beyond his own four walls was the point at which my friend began each day. He began by looking outward.

Looking upward. When my wife and I visited the little church where Shakespeare is buried in Stratford-upon-Avon, an usher handed us a sheet of paper which said, "We ask as you walk round, please to remember that you are on holy ground, to behave reverently, to restrain your speaking . . . and, if you wish to see the glory of this church, *Do not forget to look up.*" The pamphlet referred specifically to the beautiful ceiling of the church, but I took it as a reminder that *looking up* is perhaps the most important looking we do in developing the true sense of where we are.

In the confusion of our day-to-day rushing about, there will come times when life does not make much sense, when it all seems fragmented. In such moments you and I are going to want to look upward to the One who alone can take the bits and pieces of our lives, rearrange them, and return them to us in a way that does make sense and that clearly shows these fragments to have been cut from the same cloth after all.

Ever notice how often most of us use two little words *if only* to explain away our shortcomings and get ourselves off the hook? We say, "If only I had a better job," "If only I lived somewhere else or times were different." Hidden away in the Gospels is the story of a woman who said "if only" and did something about it. She had been ill for twelve years, going from doctor to doctor with no success. "If only I could touch the robe that man [Jesus] is wearing, I would be cured," she said. So she pushed her way up through the crowd. With effort, faith, and expectancy, she reached out, touched that garment, and was cured.

We reach out like that woman, but often we fail to reach far enough. The electricity, the power of God, is still there, but it is for us to reach out far enough to throw the switch. Instead of saying "if only," maybe we can learn to say with Paul and believe it right down to the soles of our feet, "I can do *all* things through Christ who strengthens me."

A Prayer for Persistence

*O Lord God, when thou givest us to endeavor any
great matter, grant us also to know that it is not the
beginning, but the continuing of the same until it
be thoroughly finished, that yieldeth the true glory;
through him who, for the finishing of thy work, lay
down his life, our Saviour Jesus Christ. Amen.*

—Sir Francis Drake
(1540-1596)

13

The Greatest Miracle
of All

ALL OF US have known times when we have worked
in behalf of some cause. We understood the issues;
we knew what to do; and we did it. We had the
glorious feeling we were accomplishing something
worthwhile. And then there have been other times
when, try as we would, nothing seemed to go right.
As Murphy's law put it, "If anything can go wrong,
it will"—and it did!

Are you consistent in the way you follow through
on projects or programs you undertake, or do you
find—as I do—that you seem to be a different person sometimes? On several occasions I have gone to
work on something I believed in deeply—raising
funds for a memorial scholarship, for example. I
started out with a bang. Then co-workers failed to

do what they said they would do. People didn't return phone calls. I became discouraged and ultimately threw in the sponge.

And there have been times when I have been irritable, fretful, or—as we like to put it—not myself at the end of a long day. I have shuffled papers, accomplishing nothing and getting nowhere. I finally say to myself, "What did it all mean? What's the use of all this futile busyness?"

All of us respond to situations, to people, and to life in different ways. Our Lord knew this and described it in the Parable of the Soils (Luke 8:4-8). People are the same today: the lighthearted have no roots; the fainthearted begin whatever they do with a grand flourish but soon lose their steam; the halfhearted are easily lured away by other influences; and the wholehearted "bring a good and honest heart to the hearing of the word, hold it fast, and, by their perseverance, yield a harvest."

Was Jesus really trying to put people into four distinct categories, or was he actually describing four different kinds of responses that he might get from any one individual at different times? Each of us may react to the same situation in different ways at different times. And I think most of us are occasionally hard of hearing when it comes to the way we respond to the Word of God.

How does God get through to us? It may be

through a sermon or that Bible on the bedside table
. . . a casual conversation with a stranger on the
bus . . . a phrase or two that jump out from an
article in the morning paper . . . a child who takes
your hand and looks up trustingly into your eyes
. . . a neighbor talks to you so forthrightly in a
way that seems out of character, but it was as if the
message came through that neighbor from our Lord
himself. It is not easy always to recognize God
speaking to us, but we can at least resolve to try not
to be hard of hearing.

In Pittsburgh some years ago, Bishop Austin Pardue was awakened by the roar of fire engines, with
their sirens screeching, rushing to a fire a block away
from his house. The bishop got up, dressed, and
hurried off to see the fire. As he started out the
door, he noticed Mrs. Pardue was sound asleep. She
had slept right through the noise, sirens and all.

After the fire was put out, the bishop came back
to bed. He found his wife still fast asleep. Nothing
had awakened her; she had slept through it all. Just
then, their little child down the hall called out softly,
"Mother!" and, like a shot, his wife was out of bed
and down the hall to check on her child. The inci-
dent reminded him that we tend to hear what we
want to hear, whether it be the cry of one's child
or the still, small voice of God.

Because my own mind has a way of closing shut

with the finality of a Mosler safe, for years I have carried in my wallet the words of a wise English-man, Leslie Weatherhead who said, "We must be openminded enough to realize that a thing may be true, even if we haven't heard of it before and may be true even if we definitely disagree with it. We must seek for truth and not just the confirmation of our preconceived ideas."

Are there false impressions, wrong ideas, deep-rooted prejudices in the soil of our lives that we can remove by consciously exposing ourselves to health-ier influences? Are there ways we can keep our of-ten selfish minds open, not closed to everything from outside? We can prepare the soil of our lives by clearing out rocks below the surface, raking up the dead leaves, and adding plant food. But God will be the sower, as George Buttrick has said, and Christ will be the seed that enables that soil of ours to yield a harvest.

All of us feel frustrated about what we have done or not done with our lives—our marriages, our homes, our families, our careers, our interpersonal relationships. We long for the transformation of seed to harvest. I once heard of a young man who felt like that and went to his vicar to ask, "How can I find the peace of God in my own life?"

"You're too late," said the clergyman.

The boy was flabbergasted. "Do you mean I'm too late to be saved?"

"No," said the pastor, "not that. I just mean that you yourself are too late to do anything about it. Jesus did it all, all that needed to be done, centuries ago, once and for all."

We can do nothing on our own. We must seek the Lord's help, tell him we want it, keep at it, and be prepared to accept it on his terms, even if it means we may be in for surprises.

It may be best for us to try saying thanks or saying we are sorry or making constructive use of silence. It may be that we shall want to be on the lookout for opportunities to further the cause of Christ even if we do not feel the transforming miracle has yet happened to us. But one day we will become conscious of the presence of someone who seems to say, "Yes it is I, and I have been here all along, waiting for you to come."

Rule of Life of the Early Christians

"And they continued steadfastly in the apostles' doctrine and fellowship, and in breaking of bread, and in prayers" (Acts 2:42).

Helps for the Layman

1. I will pretend each day is the first of my spiritual program because I am best at the beginning of a campaign.

2. I will use flash-prayers frequently throughout the day because repeated through-the-day contact with God can multiply my effectiveness immeasurably.

3. I will try to be honest in my prayers because only then do they mean anything to me and, consequently, to God. If my mind is wandering, I'll tell him so and ask his help.

4. I will pray about specific problems because such prayers will mean more to me than overly general prayers.

5. I will make a regular effort to know the Bible better, trying to see the great relevance of Christ's teachings to life today.

6. I will try winning others to Christ, not only because it was Christ's command that I do so, but also because faith seems to grow when it is shared.

7. I will try to see the human equation in everything I do, realizing how individuals are affected by every decision I make, every letter I write, and by even the most casual encounter.

8. I will ask myself at the end of the day, as George MacDonald suggests, if I have this day done anything because God said do it or abstained from doing anything because he said do not do it.

9. I will try to have a partner in my spiritual program because comparing notes with someone else can give a program wings and appreciably help both of us.

10. I will accept opportunities for service, as Albert Schweitzer suggests, with sober enthusiasm, remembering the many others, willing and able, who are not in a position to do the same.

DATE DUE

JAN 4 '78			